Demystifying Gemini AI

A Technical Deep Dive

Tech Talker

Table of contents

Introduction

The evolving landscape of artificial intelligence has been marked by the rise of large language models, transforming the way we interact with technology and pushing the boundaries of what's possible. In this dynamic realm, Google's Gemini AI emerges as a groundbreaking force, reshaping the contours of AI capabilities.

Gemini AI stands at the forefront of innovation, representing Google's latest venture into the realm of large language models (LLMs). This book is your guide to understanding the intricacies of Gemini AI, its far-reaching applications, and the transformative impact it holds in the broader context of artificial intelligence.

As we embark on this exploration, we'll unravel the historical journey of large language models, providing context to the revolutionary developments that led to the creation of Gemini. The significance of Gemini in the AI space goes beyond mere technological advancement; it signifies a paradigm shift in how we conceive and utilize language models.

Join us on this journey as we delve into the depths of Gemini AI, unlocking its potential and demystifying the complexities that make it a pivotal player in the landscape of artificial intelligence. Get ready to witness the fusion of human and AI capabilities, from coding prowess to offline brilliance, as we navigate the multifaceted facets of Google's multimodal revolution

Chapter 1:

The Evolution of Large Language Models

Historical context of large language models.

To truly grasp the revolutionary impact of Gemini AI, it's essential to rewind the tape of time and explore the historical evolution of large language models. The landscape of artificial intelligence has been shaped by incremental breakthroughs, each paving the way for the next leap in innovation.

The inception of large language models can be traced back to the early aspirations of mimicking human language understanding. Early attempts, though ambitious, grappled with limitations in processing power and data availability. However, the persistent pursuit of refining language models laid the groundwork for the monumental strides witnessed today.

As computational capabilities surged and datasets expanded, models like OpenAI's GPT series and BERT from Google showcased unprecedented language comprehension. These milestones fueled a surge in applications, from natural language processing to content generation, setting the stage for the emergence of Gemini AI.

Gemini AI, the latest entrant in this lineage, represents a culmination of advancements, surpassing its predecessors in both scale and sophistication. Its ability to seamlessly reason across text, images, video, audio, and code marks a paradigm shift in how large language models engage with and interpret diverse forms of information.

In understanding the historical context, we appreciate not just the technological milestones but the relentless pursuit of enhancing language models—a journey that brings us to the forefront of the AI revolution with Gemini.

Milestones leading up to the development of Gemini AI

The journey towards Gemini AI is punctuated by significant milestones that mark the evolution of large language models. These milestones are not mere stepping stones but pivotal moments that have collectively propelled the field of artificial intelligence to new heights.

Pioneering Language Models: The initial forays into language modeling were characterized by foundational models like ELIZA and SHRDLU. While rudimentary by today's standards, they laid the groundwork for the pursuit of advanced language understanding.

Statistical Language Processing: The advent of statistical language processing in the 1990s brought about a paradigm shift. Models like Hidden Markov Models and n-gram models demonstrated improved language understanding, fueled by statistical patterns derived from vast datasets.

Rise of Neural Networks: The resurgence of neural networks, particularly with the introduction of deep learning, sparked a revolution in natural language processing. Word embeddings, recurrent neural networks (RNNs), and long short-term memory (LSTM) networks emerged, enabling models to capture intricate linguistic nuances.

Transformer Architecture: The introduction of the Transformer architecture in 2017, as seen in models like GPT (Generative Pre-trained Transformer), revolutionized language modeling. Attention mechanisms and parallelization enhanced the efficiency of processing contextual information, leading to more coherent and context-aware responses.

Multimodal Capabilities: GPT-3, a predecessor to Gemini AI, showcased the potential of multimodal capabilities. Its ability to process and generate content across various modalities, including text, images, and code, set the stage for Gemini's groundbreaking versatility.

Gemini AI Unleashed: The unveiling of Gemini AI represents a culmination of these milestones. It surpasses its predecessors by integrating state-of-the-art techniques in language processing, leveraging vast datasets, and demonstrating unparalleled performance across a spectrum of tasks.

Understanding these milestones provides context to Gemini AI's significance, highlighting the continuous refinement and innovation that has shaped the landscape of large language models.

Chapter 2:

Under the Hood - Technical Architecture

Deep dive into the technical architecture of Gemini AI.

The intricate web of Gemini AI's technical architecture is a marvel in the realm of large language models. At its core lies a sophisticated neural network, a digital brain capable of processing and generating information with unprecedented finesse. Let's embark on a deep dive into the neural nexus that powers Gemini AI.

Transformer Framework: Gemini AI inherits the Transformer architecture, a groundbreaking framework that has become the backbone of modern language models. Within this framework, attention mechanisms play a pivotal role, allowing the model to focus on different parts of the input sequence dynamically.

Encoder-Decoder Paradigm: The architecture employs the encoder-decoder paradigm, a structural dichotomy that facilitates both understanding and generation of content. The encoder processes input data, extracting contextual information, while the decoder generates coherent and contextually relevant output.

Attention Mechanisms: Gemini AI's prowess is amplified by advanced attention mechanisms. Self-attention mechanisms enable the model to weigh the significance of different words in a sequence, capturing intricate relationships and dependencies.

Multi-head attention ensures a nuanced understanding of context.

Parameter Tuning: The success of Gemini AI is not merely attributed to its architectural blueprint but also to meticulous parameter tuning. The model's parameters, including weights and biases, undergo optimization during training, fine-tuning the neural connections to enhance performance.

Multimodal Integration: What sets Gemini AI apart is its ability to seamlessly navigate the diverse landscape of text, images, video, audio, and code. The architecture incorporates multimodal integration, allowing the model to process and generate content across multiple modalities cohesively.

Continuous Learning: Gemini AI exhibits a form of continuous learning, refining its understanding over time. Through exposure to vast datasets and iterative training processes, the model adapts to evolving linguistic nuances and contextual intricacies.

Resource Utilization: The architecture is designed for efficient resource utilization, enabling Gemini AI to execute complex tasks with speed and precision. This optimization is particularly evident in its ability to handle large-scale training on specialized hardware like Google's Tensor Processing Units (TPUs).

As we unravel the technical intricacies of Gemini AI's architecture, it becomes evident that its design is not just a culmination of algorithms but a symphony of neural orchestration, harmonizing diverse elements to redefine the frontiers of artificial intelligence.

Key components and their functions

Within the labyrinthine structure of Gemini AI's architecture, distinct components act as maestros, conducting the symphony of intelligence. Each component serves a unique function, contributing to the model's unparalleled capabilities. Let's dissect these key components and unravel their roles in orchestrating Gemini AI's intelligence.

Encoder Unit:

Function: The encoder acts as the model's sensory system, absorbing input data and converting it into a format the model can comprehend.

Role: Capturing the essence of input sequences, the encoder generates contextual embeddings that form the foundation for subsequent processing.

Decoder Unit:

Function: Operating in tandem with the encoder, the decoder interprets the contextual embeddings and transforms them into coherent and meaningful output.

Role: *Responsible for the generation of text, code, or responses, the decoder infuses intelligence into the model's output.*

Attention Mechanisms:

Function: *Attention mechanisms enable Gemini AI to selectively focus on specific parts of input sequences, mimicking human attention.*

Role: *By assigning different weights to different elements, attention mechanisms empower the model to grasp intricate relationships and dependencies.*

Self-Attention Mechanisms:

Function: *A subset of attention mechanisms, self-attention allows the* model to weigh the importance of individual words within a sequence.

Role: Enhancing the model's ability to understand context, self-attention refines its grasp on nuanced linguistic nuances.

Multi-Head Attention:

Function: Multi-head attention extends the model's capacity to consider multiple perspectives simultaneously.

Role: By leveraging diverse attention heads, the model gains a holistic understanding of complex relationships within and across sequences.

Parameter Tuning:

Function: *Parameters, including weights and biases, undergo dynamic adjustments during training to optimize the model's performance.*

Role: *Fine-tuning parameters ensures that the model refines its neural connections, adapting to evolving datasets and linguistic patterns.*

Multimodal Integration:

Function: *Gemini AI's ability to process text, images, video, audio, and code seamlessly is facilitated by multimodal integration.*

Role: *Integrating information across modalities enables the model to generate diverse and contextually relevant outputs.*

Continuous Learning Mechanism:

Function: *Gemini AI adopts a continuous learning approach, refining its understanding over successive exposures to vast datasets.*

Role: *The model adapts to evolving linguistic nuances and contextual intricacies, ensuring its intelligence remains abreast of real-world dynamics.*

Resource Management Unit:

Function: *Optimizing resource utilization, this unit ensures efficient execution of tasks, particularly during large-scale training on Tensor Processing Units (TPUs).*

Role: *By leveraging specialized hardware, Gemini AI achieves enhanced speed and precision in executing complex computations.*

Understanding these key components unveils the inner workings of Gemini AI, portraying how each element contributes to the model's prowess in processing information and generating intelligent outputs across diverse domains.

Chapter 3:
Training and Learning Mechanisms

The training process on Google's Tensor Processing Units (TPU)

In the grand orchestration of Gemini AI's evolution, the training process takes center stage, conducted by the virtuoso known as Tensor Processing Units (TPUs). This segment unveils the meticulous dance between Gemini AI and TPUs, elucidating how this collaboration achieves unparalleled speed and precision in molding the model's intelligence.

TPU Architecture Overview:

- Harmony of Hardware: Google's Tensor Processing Units are custom accelerators designed specifically for machine learning tasks, orchestrating a harmonious interplay between hardware and software.

- Parallel Processing Power: TPUs excel in parallel processing, managing multiple tasks simultaneously and accelerating the training of large language models like Gemini AI.

Massive Datasets and Optimization Algorithms:

- Data as the Score: The training process commences with the ingestion of vast datasets, akin to providing the musical score for Gemini AI's symphony.

- Algorithmic Choreography: Optimization algorithms choreograph the learning journey, guiding the model through intricate patterns and refining its understanding with each iteration.

Pre-training and Fine-tuning Techniques:

- Pre-training Prelude: Gemini AI undergoes pre-training, an initial phase where it learns the nuances of language from extensive datasets, akin to a musical prelude setting the tone.

- Fine-tuning Symphony: Fine-tuning refines the model's acumen for specific tasks, akin to adjusting musical nuances to suit different compositions and genres.

Data Quality and Diversity:

- Harmonizing Diversity: The quality and diversity of training data play a pivotal role, shaping Gemini AI's adaptability to a spectrum of linguistic intricacies.

- Tuning to Real-world Dynamics: Exposure to diverse datasets ensures that the model attunes itself to the dynamic symphony of real-world language, avoiding monotony and bias.

Dynamic Parameter Adjustments:

- Precision in Performance: Parameters, the notes in Gemini AI's neural composition, undergo dynamic adjustments during training, fine-tuning the model's performance with each iteration.

- Adaptation to Complexity: The model refines its neural connections, akin to a musician adapting to the complexity of a musical composition.

Efficient Resource Utilization:

- TPU as the Conductor: TPUs orchestrate the training process with efficiency, managing resources to ensure a seamless and swift performance.

- Symphony of Speed: The specialized hardware ensures not only precision but also accelerates the training, transforming Gemini AI into a high-speed virtuoso.

The training process on Tensor Processing Units epitomizes the collaboration between cutting-edge hardware and advanced algorithms, sculpting Gemini AI into a model of exceptional intelligence. This synergy between technology and technique creates a symphony of speed and precision, propelling Gemini AI to the forefront of the artificial intelligence landscape.

How Gemini AI learns from diverse datasets

Gemini AI, Google's avant-garde large language model, doesn't just learn; it orchestrates a symphony of intelligence by embracing the rich diversity of datasets. In this chapter, we unravel the notes of this melodic journey, exploring how Gemini AI extracts knowledge, nuances, and linguistic subtleties from a kaleidoscope of data sources.

Ingesting a Mosaic of Textual Patterns:

- The Prelude: Gemini AI embarks on its learning journey with a prelude, absorbing vast amounts of text data from an eclectic array of sources.

- Diverse Genres: Textual data spans genres, from literature and news articles to social media posts, allowing Gemini AI to comprehend language intricacies across diverse contexts.

Visual Harmony through Image-Text Integration:

- Multimodal Symphony: Gemini AI extends its capabilities beyond text, incorporating the visual dimension through image-text integration.

- Images as Melodic Threads: The model learns to associate textual descriptions with visual content, harmonizing language understanding with image recognition.

Auditory Nuances in Audio Data:

- Aural Comprehension: Beyond text and images, Gemini AI extends its repertoire to audio data, decoding spoken words, tones, and contextual nuances.

- The Rhythmic Flow: Exposure to diverse voices and speech patterns refines Gemini AI's ability to interpret and generate human-like responses in audio interactions.

Synchronized Learning from Code:

- Coding Cadence: Gemini AI's prowess extends to understanding and generating code, synchronizing its learning from diverse coding languages and structures.

- Algorithmic Harmony: Exposure to an array of coding styles allows Gemini AI to compose code snippets with fluency and adaptability.

Cultural and Linguistic Diversity:

- Global Linguistic Palette: Gemini AI navigates the linguistic mosaic of different languages, enriching its understanding of cultural nuances and linguistic diversity.

- Adapting to Vernaculars: Regional idioms, colloquialisms, and vernacular expressions become integral elements in Gemini AI's linguistic repertoire.

Real-world Contextual Awareness:

- Contextual Symphony: Gemini AI is trained on datasets reflecting real-world scenarios, ensuring it captures the dynamic interplay of language within various contexts.

- Social and Ethical Nuances: Exposure to diverse contexts fosters an awareness of social and ethical nuances, contributing to responsible and context-aware language generation.

As Gemini AI traverses the diverse landscapes of textual, visual, auditory, and coding data, it composes a symphony of intelligence that resonates with the richness and complexity of the real world. This chapter unveils the intricacies of Gemini AI's multifaceted learning approach, showcasing how its melody is finely tuned to the diverse notes of the global information symphony.

Chapter 4:

Gemini's Multimodal Capabilities

In-depth analysis of Gemini's ability to process text, images, video, audio, and code

In the grand symphony of artificial intelligence, Gemini AI emerges as a virtuoso, capable of interpreting the nuanced languages of diverse data modalities. This chapter unravels the narrative of Gemini's Multimodal Mastery, showcasing its prowess in seamlessly processing text, images, video, audio, and code.

1. Textual Symphony: Beyond Words

As Gemini delves into textual processing, it goes beyond the mere understanding of words. Its proficiency extends to deciphering the subtleties of language, grasping contextual nuances, and even discerning the underlying sentiments. The result is an advanced language comprehension that sets Gemini apart.

2. Visual Rhapsody: Decoding Visual Narratives

Venturing into the visual domain, Gemini displays a remarkable ability to process and understand images. It decodes visual narratives, showcasing an integration of textual and visual information that creates a harmonious fusion of meaning. The result is a comprehensive understanding that mirrors human-like perception.

3. Cinematic Understanding: Video Comprehension Mastery

Gemini's capabilities extend to the dynamic realm of video content. It navigates through scenes, identifies objects, and comprehends actions, showcasing a mastery of video comprehension. Temporal awareness further enhances its ability to understand and respond to the evolving visual narratives presented in video data.

4. Sonic Sophistication: Auditory Perception

In the auditory realm, Gemini proves its sophistication by processing spoken words, tones, and ambient sounds. It exhibits an in-depth understanding of auditory information, showcasing the model's ability to discern spoken language and contextual nuances within diverse soundscapes.

5. Code as a Compositional Language: Coding Maestro

Embracing the language of code, Gemini showcases its coding prowess across various programming languages. It acts as a coding maestro, generating coherent and syntactically accurate code snippets. This capability opens new avenues for human-machine coding collaboration, marking a significant stride in the fusion of AI and software development.

Real-world applications and use cases.

Embarking on a voyage through the real-world applications of Gemini AI, we discover a transformative force that transcends theoretical prowess. This chapter navigates the tangible realms where

Gemini's capabilities manifest, leaving an indelible mark across various industries.

1. Healthcare Harmonies: Personalized Care and Biosensor Integration

In the healthcare domain, Gemini proves to be a guardian of well-being. Through personalized healthcare applications, it analyzes vast datasets to tailor medical insights, providing individuals with a nuanced understanding of their health. Additionally, Gemini seamlessly integrates with biosensors, augmenting the diagnostic process and laying the foundation for proactive health management.

2. Geospatial Symphony: Multisource Data Fusion and Continuous Monitoring

Gemini's impact reverberates in geospatial science, orchestrating a symphony of data fusion, planning, and intelligence. It navigates through multisource data, offering unprecedented insights for urban planning, disaster response, and continuous monitoring. The result is a harmonized approach to geospatial analysis that transforms how we perceive and interact with our environment.

3. Tech Fusion: Domain Knowledge Transfer and Enhanced Decision-Making

In the realm of integrated technologies, Gemini acts as a catalyst for knowledge transfer. It facilitates the seamless transfer of domain knowledge, enhancing decision-making processes across industries. This fusion of AI capabilities with domain-specific expertise signifies a paradigm shift, empowering organizations to make informed and impactful choices.

4. CodeCraft: AlphaCode 2's Triumph in Coding Competitions

Unveiling its coding prowess, Gemini takes center stage in coding competitions with AlphaCode 2. Surpassing human competitors, this application demonstrates Gemini's ability to generate high-quality, competitive code. The fusion of human creativity and AI precision marks a milestone in the evolution of coding practices.

As we traverse these real-world landscapes, the multifaceted impact of Gemini AI becomes apparent. From revolutionizing healthcare practices to harmonizing geospatial analyses, facilitating tech-driven decision-making, and triumphing in coding competitions, Gemini's applications transcend the theoretical realm. The pages of this chapter unfold a narrative of tangible, transformative change, positioning Gemini as a cornerstone in the ever-evolving tapestry of artificial intelligence.

Chapter 5:

Challenges and Solutions

The technical challenges in explaining
complex AI concepts

Navigating the intricacies of large language models and artificial intelligence can be akin to deciphering an intricate code. As we embark on this journey to unravel the mysteries behind Gemini AI, it's imperative to acknowledge the technical challenges inherent in articulating the complexities of cutting-edge AI concepts.

The field of artificial intelligence has witnessed unprecedented advancements, paving the way for large language models that transcend conventional boundaries. Gemini AI, standing at the forefront of this revolution, beckons us to delve into its intricate technical architecture—a terrain often characterized by intricate components and sophisticated algorithms.

To appreciate the significance of Gemini AI, we must first grasp the historical context that has shaped the landscape of large language models. Milestones leading up to the development of Gemini AI mark pivotal moments in the evolution of artificial intelligence, laying the foundation for the groundbreaking capabilities we are set to explore.

As we unravel the layers of Gemini AI's technical architecture, we'll encounter a sophisticated framework comprising key components, each with a unique function contributing to the model's prowess. This deep dive will illuminate the inner workings of Gemini, shedding light on its transformative power in processing diverse data modalities.

The journey extends beyond the static realms of architecture into the dynamic realm of training. Gemini AI's education on Google's Tensor Processing Units (TPU) is a critical chapter, revealing the model's ability to learn from extensive and diverse datasets. This process, akin to the model's intellectual evolution, is a fascinating exploration of machine learning's inner sanctum.

A cornerstone of Gemini AI's capabilities lies in its multifaceted approach to processing various forms of information—text, images, video, audio, and code. This capability transcends traditional boundaries, positioning Gemini as a versatile force with real-world applications that span a multitude of industries.

Yet, in our pursuit of understanding, we must acknowledge the challenges posed by translating complex AI concepts into digestible narratives. The technical intricacies demand a delicate balance between depth and clarity, a challenge we embrace as we navigate this realm of cutting-edge technology.

As we navigate through this labyrinth of technical challenges, our goal is to demystify Gemini AI, making its complexities accessible to a broad audience. The journey promises to be intellectually rewarding, offering insights into the heart of artificial intelligence and the transformative power of large language models. Let the exploration commence.

Strategies for making technical content accessible to a broader audience

In our quest to unveil the intricacies of Gemini AI, we encounter a challenge—making the intricate dance of technical concepts accessible to a broader audience. The journey thus far has immersed us in the depths of large language models and artificial intelligence, but our commitment extends beyond comprehension within specialized circles. We now venture into the realm of strategies aimed at bridging the gap between technical complexity and broader accessibility.

The very essence of this pursuit lies in recognizing that the allure of Gemini AI should not be confined to the elite echelons of technical expertise. It beckons us to develop strategies that render its complexities comprehensible to a diverse audience with varying degrees of technical familiarity.

One fundamental strategy involves contextualizing the technical architecture of Gemini AI within a broader narrative. Rather than drowning in the sea of technical jargon, we aim to craft a storyline that captivates and educates. The historical evolution of large language models becomes a gripping saga, setting the stage for Gemini AI as the protagonist in an unfolding AI narrative.

Another pivotal approach revolves around the demystification of key technical components. The labyrinthine layers of Gemini's architecture, adorned with terms like Transformer models, encoders, decoders, and attention mechanisms, demand a nuanced yet accessible explanation. Analogies, metaphors, and relatable comparisons become our tools, transforming complexity into clarity.

Training, a core chapter in Gemini's story, invites us to elucidate the learning process without overwhelming the reader. The journey on Google's Tensor Processing

Units becomes a guided tour rather than an impenetrable maze. We traverse the landscapes of extensive datasets, decoding the model's education in a language that transcends technical barriers.

The versatility of Gemini AI, extending beyond text to embrace images, video, audio, and code, necessitates a strategy that accentuates its real-world applications. We navigate this terrain with concrete examples, case studies, and relatable scenarios that paint a vivid picture of Gemini's impact on diverse industries.

Acknowledging the challenge of translating technical intricacies into accessible narratives, we embrace a commitment to clarity. Every chapter becomes a quest for the delicate balance between depth and simplicity. The goal is not merely to present information but to craft an engaging narrative that beckons readers, regardless of their technical background.

As we lay out these strategies, we invite you to join us on this endeavor. Gemini AI, with its transformative potential, deserves to transcend the confines of technical enclaves. Together, we embark on a journey to make the complex accessible, ensuring that the brilliance of Gemini shines through for all to witness.

Chapter 6:

The Impact of Gemini AI

Gemini's impact on various industries

In the realm of healthcare, Gemini emerges as a silent revolutionary, wielding its prowess in personalized healthcare, biosensor integration, and preventative medicine. The model's ability to navigate the intricacies of health-related data opens new frontiers for personalized treatments and diagnostic precision. We witness Gemini's foray into a domain where every bit of information holds the potential to enhance the quality of human life.

The integration of Gemini AI into the fabric of integrated technologies is a testament to its role as a catalyst for domain knowledge transfer, data fusion, and enhanced decision-making. Across industries, from finance to manufacturing, Gemini becomes the silent partner in augmenting human decision-making processes. The synergy between artificial intelligence and human expertise reaches new heights, ushering in an era of unprecedented collaboration.

As we traverse the landscapes of geospatial science, Gemini's role in multisource data fusion, planning, and intelligence unfolds. The model's capacity for continuous monitoring charts a new course in spatial analysis, where real-time insights become the bedrock for informed decision-making. The boundaries between physical and digital realities blur as Gemini establishes itself as a linchpin in geospatial advancements.

The impact of Gemini on coding experiences takes center stage with the introduction of AlphaCode 2. In the competitive arena of coding competitions, Gemini's prowess shines, outperforming participants and raising the bar for what is achievable. We witness the evolution of coding as Gemini elevates the standards, proving that artificial intelligence can not only assist but also excel in the creative and intricate realm of coding.

The journey into Gemini's impact on the coding landscape brings us to the unveiling of Google's new code-generating system, AlphaCode 2. Here, Gemini's capabilities transcend mere assistance, positioning it as a formidable force in coding competitions. The narrative unfolds with a sense of anticipation as we explore how AlphaCode 2 redefines the benchmarks in coding prowess.

In the domain of computer vision, Gemini takes center stage, showcasing its capabilities in object detection, scene understanding, and anomaly detection. The lens through which Gemini perceives and interprets visual data becomes a focal point, unveiling a new era in computer vision where artificial intelligence stands as a visionary companion in deciphering the visual complexities of the world.

The narrative expands into the realm of Tensor Processing Units (TPUs), offering insights into the significance of Gemini's training on TPU for enhanced speed and cost-effectiveness. The interplay between

Gemini and TPU becomes a critical juncture in the story, demonstrating how hardware optimization elevates the model's efficiency to unprecedented levels.

As we explore these dimensions of Gemini's impact, the overarching theme emerges—the model's transformative influence is not confined to a singular industry or application. Instead, it weaves a tapestry that connects healthcare, technology integration, geospatial science, coding competitions, computer vision, and hardware optimization. The story of Gemini's impact becomes a testament to the model's versatility and its potential to reshape the technological landscape across diverse domains.

Chapter 7:

Future Trends and Developments

Predictions and Speculations on the Future of Large Language Models

As we peer into the horizon of artificial intelligence, the future of large language models like Gemini AI unfolds with limitless possibilities. The trajectory of these models hints at a transformative impact across various domains, sparking conversations about what lies ahead.

Envisioning the Future Landscape

The road ahead is paved with innovation and advancements. Industry experts speculate that large language models will become integral to reshaping the way we interact with technology. From more sophisticated natural language understanding to enhanced problem-solving capabilities, Gemini AI foreshadows a future where human-AI collaboration takes center stage.

Industries on the Verge of Transformation

1. Healthcare: Anticipated breakthroughs include personalized diagnostics, drug discovery, and AI-assisted medical decision-making. Gemini AI's potential to analyze vast datasets may lead to more accurate diagnoses and treatment recommendations.

2. Education: The future classroom could witness a revolution, with AI-powered tutors providing personalized learning experiences. Gemini AI might facilitate

better understanding, engagement, and adaptation to individual student needs.

3. Business and Finance: Enhanced natural language processing may reshape financial analytics and decision-making. Gemini AI could prove invaluable in sifting through vast volumes of financial data, offering insights for more informed business strategies.

4. Creativity and Content Creation: We might witness a surge in AI-generated content, from writing and music composition to visual arts. Gemini AI's ability to understand context and generate coherent, creative output opens doors to new possibilities in the entertainment and creative industries.

Ethical Considerations

However, with great power comes great responsibility. As we embark on this AI-driven future, ethical considerations become paramount. Questions about biases, transparency, and the responsible deployment of large language models must be carefully addressed to ensure a future that benefits society as a whole.

Looking Beyond

While we're only at the cusp of this transformative journey, the potential impact of Gemini AI on our future is both exciting and challenging. Only time will unveil the true extent of its influence on our lives, industries, and the evolving landscape of artificial intelligence.

Considerations for staying updated in this rapidly evolving field

Navigating the rapidly evolving landscape of artificial intelligence, especially in the realm of large language models, requires a strategic approach to staying informed. As Gemini AI and its counterparts continue to advance, enthusiasts, professionals, and curious minds alike must adopt effective strategies to keep abreast of the latest developments.

The Pursuit of Knowledge: A Continuous Journey

1. Diversify Your Sources: Cast a wide net when seeking information. Follow reputable journals, research papers, and

industry publications. Diversifying your sources ensures a holistic understanding of the field.

2. Engage in Online Communities: Join forums, discussion groups, and social media communities dedicated to AI and large language models. Engaging in conversations with peers, researchers, and practitioners provides valuable insights and updates.

3. Attend Conferences and Webinars: Participate in conferences, workshops, and webinars related to artificial intelligence. These events offer opportunities to hear from experts, witness live demonstrations, and gain

firsthand knowledge about the latest advancements.

4. Subscribe to Newsletters: Stay informed with regular newsletters from AI research organizations, tech companies, and thought leaders. Newsletters often curate key developments, making it easier to stay updated without being overwhelmed.

5. Continuous Learning: Invest time in continuous learning. Online platforms offer courses, tutorials, and certifications in artificial intelligence. Platforms like Coursera, edX, and others provide a structured learning environment.

Embracing Collaboration and Networking

1. Collaborate with Peers: Foster collaboration with fellow enthusiasts, researchers, and professionals. Participating in collaborative projects or research initiatives allows for shared learning experiences and diverse perspectives.

2. Networking Events: Attend local or virtual networking events within the AI community. Networking provides opportunities to exchange ideas, discuss trends, and establish connections with like-minded individuals.

3. Mentorship: Seek mentorship from experienced professionals in the field.

Having a mentor can provide guidance, insights, and a roadmap for navigating the complexities of AI research and development.

Adapting to Change

1. Be Adaptive: Embrace change as an inherent part of the AI landscape. New models, algorithms, and techniques emerge regularly. Being adaptable ensures that you can quickly incorporate new knowledge into your understanding.

2. Experiment and Apply: Hands-on experience is invaluable. Experiment with AI frameworks, build projects, and apply theoretical knowledge to practical scenarios. Learning by doing enhances comprehension and skill development.

In a field as dynamic as artificial intelligence, the commitment to lifelong learning and a proactive approach to staying informed are keys to unlocking the full potential of Gemini AI and other advancements in the world of large language models.

Conclusion

In the tapestry of artificial intelligence, where every thread represents an advancement, Gemini AI emerges as a vibrant hue, weaving together a story of innovation and limitless possibilities.

As we wrap up our journey through the intricacies of Gemini AI, imagine a world where machines understand not just words, but the essence of human communication. Picture a landscape where Gemini's gaze extends beyond language, encompassing the rich tapestry of images, videos, audio, and the intricate patterns of code.

In the realm of computer vision, Gemini paints vivid pictures with its unparalleled capabilities in object detection, scene understanding, and anomaly detection. It's not just processing information; it's perceiving the world in a way that bridges the gap between artificial intelligence and human intuition.

Venture into the realm of geospatial science, where Gemini's role extends beyond data fusion to planning, intelligence, and continuous monitoring. The digital cartographer that Gemini becomes unfolds maps not just of terrain but of opportunities for enhanced decision-making and strategic insights.

Now, let's journey into the corridors of human health, where Gemini delicately balances the scales of personalized healthcare, biosensor integration, and preventative medicine. It's not just about data; it's about crafting a narrative of well-being, where every individual becomes a character in the story of their health.

In the symphony of integrated technologies, Gemini conducts the orchestra of domain knowledge transfer, data fusion, and enhanced decision-making. It's not just processing; it's orchestrating a harmonious blend of expertise and information to compose a melody of efficiency.

Picture AlphaCode 2 stepping onto the coding stage, unveiling a new era in programming prowess. Gemini's influence echoes through coding competitions, not just as a participant but as a frontrunner, transforming the coding landscape with precision and ingenuity.

As we navigate the chapters of Nano, Pro, and Ultra variants, we uncover a spectrum of possibilities tailored to diverse user needs. It's not just about technology; it's about crafting an experience that aligns with the unique requirements and aspirations of every user.

In the grand finale, Gemini AI stands not just as a model but as a testament to the boundless potential of artificial intelligence. The story continues, and the future chapters are yet unwritten. Your role in this narrative is pivotal—embracing curiosity, staying engaged, and being part of the ongoing saga of innovation.

As we conclude this chapter, remember, the tapestry of Gemini AI is not static; it's a living, evolving canvas. Your journey with Gemini is not just an exploration; it's a collaborative creation of the future—a future where the language of AI speaks fluently to the aspirations of humanity.